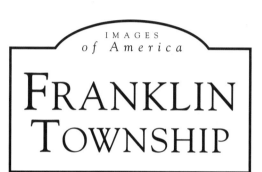

IMAGES
of America

# FRANKLIN
# TOWNSHIP

CELEBRATING 200 YEARS

FRANKLIN TOWNSHIP

1798 - 1998

IMAGES
*of America*

# FRANKLIN
# TOWNSHIP

William Brahms
and the Franklin Township Public Library

ARCADIA

First published 1997
Copyright © William Brahms and the Franklin Township Public Library, 1997

ISBN 0-7524-0938-7

Published by Arcadia Publishing,
an imprint of the Chalford Publishing Corporation,
One Washington Center, Dover, New Hampshire 03820.
Printed in Great Britain

Library of Congress Cataloging-in-Publication Data applied for

# Contents

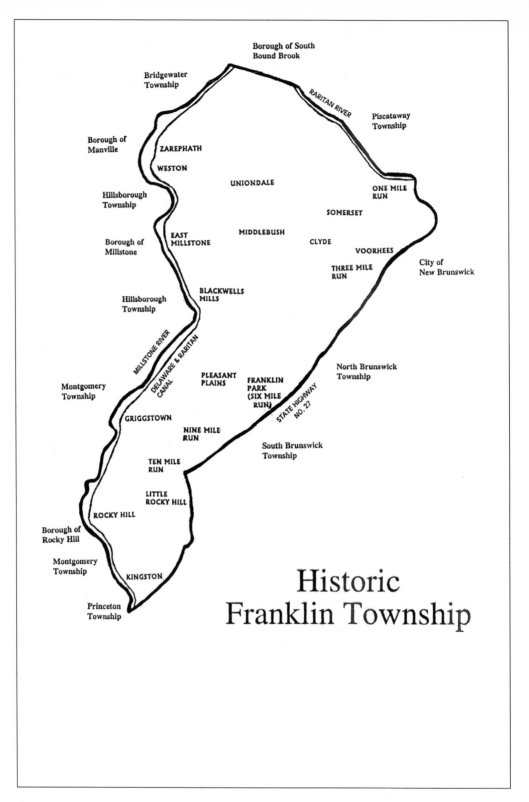

Borough of South
Bound Brook

Bridgewater
Township

RARITAN RIVER

Piscataway
Township

Borough of
Manville

ZAREPHATH

WESTON

UNIONDALE

ONE MILE
RUN

Hillsborough
Township

SOMERSET

Borough of
Millstone

EAST
MILLSTONE

MIDDLEBUSH

CLYDE

VOORHEES

City of
New Brunswick

THREE MILE
RUN

Hillsborough
Township

BLACKWELLS
MILLS

MILLSTONE RIVER

DELAWARE & RARITAN CANAL

Montgomery
Township

PLEASANT
PLAINS

FRANKLIN
PARK
(SIX MILE
RUN)

North Brunswick
Township

GRIGGSTOWN

STATE HIGHWAY
NO. 27

NINE MILE
RUN

South Brunswick
Township

TEN MILE
RUN

LITTLE
ROCKY HILL

ROCKY HILL

Borough of
Rocky Hill

Montgomery
Township

KINGSTON

Princeton
Township

# Historic
# Franklin Township

# Introduction

Franklin Township is in southeastern Somerset County in central New Jersey. The township's approximately 47 square miles form an elongated triangle, with the Raritan and the Millstone Rivers delineating most of two sides; Route 27 marks the third. Franklin is situated midway on what some writers call the "waist" of New Jersey—a line that marks the shortest distance between Philadelphia and New York.

Incorporated in 1798, Franklin is the governing municipality for more than 45,000 people. Within its boundaries are several villages, including Blackwells Mills, East Millstone, Franklin Park, Griggstown, Kingston, Middlebush, Somerset, and Zarephath. Although parts of Franklin have remained refreshingly rural going into the twenty-first century, the township could never be called remote. Franklin is within commuting distance of both the Philadelphia and New York metropolitan areas and it is a much shorter hop to several world-class universities, including Princeton and Rutgers.

Settlement of Franklin Township started in the 1680s along the Raritan River, with the Raritan Lots. In 1701, the 10,000-acre Harrison Tract was developed south of the Raritan Lots. The Dutch investors who bought land in the Raritan Lots, Harrison Tract, and elsewhere in Franklin formed the largest group of early township settlers. They were typically third- and fourth-generation colonists from New York.

The Dutch had a tremendous impact on the early development of the township. This is evident in the Dutch architecture, the overwhelming number of early Dutch surnames, and the rise of the Dutch Reformed church. But among the early settlers were also some French and Germans. The French were Huguenots and Walloons who fled to America to escape religious persecution. The Germans from the Palatinate also came to America for religious freedom.

While the Dutch descendants were settling Franklin near New Brunswick, the offspring of English colonists from New England were finding new homes in southern Franklin near Princeton. The English influence is seen in English surnames and in the emergence of the Presbyterian church in Kingston.

African-Americans have had a strong presence in Franklin since the very early 1700s. With few exceptions, labor on the farms of early Dutch settlers of Franklin and elsewhere in East Jersey was provided by black slaves. Many former slaves remained in the township's villages after manumission.

In colonial times, a major Native American path along Franklin Township's eastern border evolved into the King's Highway—the primary road between New York and Philadelphia. The highway, today's Route 27, was used by a steady stream of stagecoaches and wagons carting passengers and goods between America's two largest cities. During the American Revolution, Franklin was crisscrossed many times by both American and British troops. Two fateful decisions were made in the township that determined the direction of the war. At Kingston in January of 1777, after the battles of Princeton and Trenton, George Washington decided not to attempt to capture British-held New Brunswick; instead, he took his war-weary troops into winter quarters in Morristown, New Jersey. For five days in June of 1777, General Cornwallis and the British army occupied Franklin and engaged in a standoff with Washington, waiting for the Continental Army in nearby Middlebrook to make a move. Washington won the waiting game, and the British pulled out of New Jersey.

In 1834, the Delaware and Raritan Canal opened along 22 miles of Franklin's western and northern borders. The railroad arrived soon afterward. Until 1850, Franklin claimed the land on which Rutgers College was located. South Bound Brook was part of Franklin until 1869.

Franklin Township was primarily an agricultural community until the early twentieth century. The population remained fairly stable until after World War I. Franklin, like many communities, felt the impact of automobiles beginning in the 1920s. Northeastern Franklin started to be developed. After World War II, Franklin, like many communities, experienced a growth spurt. The population leaped in one decade by almost 107 percent to 9,858 in 1960.

With the opening of Route 287, Franklin began attracting national and international businesses to its new industrial parks. Today, corporate giants such as Merrill Lynch, AT&T, Cosmair, Philips, Brothers International, and Federal Express are major employers in the township. The Garden State Exhibit Center—one of the largest spots for conventions and exhibitions in the state—opened in Franklin in 1990.

Franklin has several interesting and very diverse claims to fame—a Revolutionary spy, Washington's sojourn, a giant, the pioneer station for transoceanic radio transmission, and one of America's most sensational murders—all of which are described on the following pages.

Franklin takes great pride in its historic structures. East Millstone, Griggstown, Rocky Hill, and Kingston have historic districts that are on the National and New Jersey Historic Registers. The Delaware and Raritan Canal Historic District, the Meadows, Rockingham, and Six Mile Run Historic District are also included on both registers.

Franklin is equally proud of its open spaces. Thirteen of its rural roads that showcase thousands of acres of farmlands and woodlands have been designated scenic corridors. The township encompasses the William L. Hutcheson Memorial Forest, perhaps the finest primeval forest on the East Coast. Colonial Park, a county park, has an arboretum, public gardens, a nature trail, and much more. The Delaware and Raritan Canal State Park has three access points in the township. Franklin's 95-acre Bunker Hill Environmental Center offers residents a first-hand opportunity to observe its forests, streams, wetlands, and other natural features.

# One
# Down on the Farm

EAST MILLSTONE DAIRY FARM, *c.* 1912.

DUTCH BARRACK, EARLY 1900s. The earliest settlers in Franklin used barracks similar to this one on Matthew Suydam's farm at Three Mile Run. Their ancestors brought the hay storage method from Holland. Each post had a series of holes. Long pins were placed in the holes to adjust the roof to the desired height. Barracks faded from use by the early 1900s as farmers turned to more efficient hay sheds.

SIMON WYCKOFF FARMSTEAD, EARLY 1900s. Farmers placed their barns a safe distance from the farmhouse because of the constant threat of fire. Dry materials such as straw stored in closed, airless buildings could cause spontaneous combustion. In the days before Franklin's volunteer fire companies, bucket brigades were useless in fighting the intense flames of a barn fire. The barns usually burned to the ground.

DUTCH BARN, 1904. John Smith's barn on Route 27 near Nine Mile Run (above) is typical of Dutch barns built by early Franklin farmers. They were distinguished by their large size, low eaves, long rafters, and great beams. When Swedish naturalist Peter Kalm traveled through the area in the 1740s, he compared their size to that of a church. Many of Franklin's Dutch barns have since disappeared, but some fine examples still stand, like the one shown below, adapted to today's uses.

LAST OF THE MOWERS, EARLY 1900s. Harvesting small grains was probably the toughest chore for Franklin farmers. Al Lewis, his sons, and McCabe used the scythes they are holding to cut the wheat. Workers followed them in the fields, gathered the wheat, and tied it into sheaves, using several stalks of the wheat to bind it together.

WHEAT HARVEST, EARLY 1900s. Bound sheaves of wheat were placed on end and piled into shocks. A few sheaves were laid across the top of the shock to serve as a cover. Later, another farm crew gathered the sheaves and either stored them in a barn or in a barrack until threshing time. A threshing machine—powered by a horse on a treadmill—removed the grain from the wheat.

MECHANIZED FARMING, *c.* 1909. The task of harvesting grain got much easier when motor-driven threshers were introduced. The work could now be done in the fields instead of the barns. This photograph shows workers at the hay press in East Millstone.

HUSKING CORN IN FRANKLIN PARK, 1904. Martin S. Garretson took hundreds of superb photographs of people and places in Franklin Township in the early 1900s. This time, he was on the other side of the camera. Garretson was the author of *The Bison of America*. He once rode a pony from Texas to South Dakota and then home to Franklin Park.

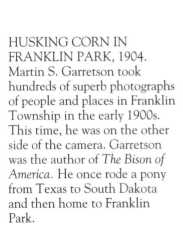

PLOWING THE FIELDS, 1904. Franklin Park farmer John Garretson's house is visible in the distance on the opposite side of Route 27. Farming was a way of life before World War I. But after the war, Franklin's farmers found they had to become more efficient, more specialized, and more market-driven. Horses and plows gave way to gas-driven tractors.

GAS-DRIVEN TRACTOR, c. 1930s. After World War I, horse-drawn plows became a rarity in Franklin. Farmers found tractors were faster and more economical. The Harold Wade farm in Middlebush, shown here, was north of Amwell Road and west of DeMott, near land that today is the site of Franklin's Municipal Complex.

14

SPLIT-RAIL FENCE, SOUTH MIDDLEBUSH ROAD, EARLY 1900s. Franklin farms had to be enclosed to keep animals from destroying the crops. Split-rail—or post-and-rail—fences were popular. They were neat and used less wood than other fences. But they took more time to build and required more upkeep. Posts were often squared, and holes had to be chiseled to hold the rails in place.

J. VAN CLEEF VOORHEES FARM, 1904. The first barns in Franklin had thatched roofs and dirt floors. Later, shingles were used on the roofs. Clapboard siding, like the kind shown here at Sleepy Hollow in Franklin Park, was widely used. Generally, the outbuildings were very dark inside. Small windows usually were used only at the roof peaks.

POULTRY RAISING, 1904. John L. Suydam is feeding geese on his Franklin Park farm in the picture above. Geese were popular on early Dutch farms, but by the late nineteenth century, advances in poultry breeding saw farmers raising less of them and more chickens. Below, Mrs. John L. Suydam feeds her chickens. Most farmers had chickens merely as a sideline to supply the eggs and meat their families needed. Serious poultry production in Franklin began in the 1930s along Davidson Avenue in the northwestern part of town and lasted until the 1960s.

F.W. REMSEN'S STORE, EAST MILLSTONE, c. 1909. Frank Remsen catered to the farming community, selling items such as hay, grain, feed, lime, cement, seeds, and fertilizers. As farming declined in the area, so did the infrastructure of services that once supported an agricultural economy. Today, Franklin farmers must travel beyond the township, and sometimes out of the state, to find needed equipment, parts, and mills to grind their grain.

LITTLE HELPER, 1904. John Howard Voorhees, son of John A. Voorhees of Pleasant Plains, rests after gathering a wagonload of firewood. Many farmers set aside wood lots—special stands of trees—that they used just for fuel. Daisy express wagons with uneven wheel sizes, like the one young John is sitting on, became popular after the Civil War and were sold until after World War I.

MILES SMITH'S WHISKEY DISTILLERY, 1904. This ancient building once housed the still of early settler Dollens Hegeman. Ten Mile Run Brook crossed a few feet from there, near the Old Road/Kings Highway (Route 27). The log in the lower center of the picture served as a footbridge.

MATTHEW SUYDAM'S SUMMER KITCHEN, FRANKLIN PARK, EARLY 1900s. In warmer weather, cooking was often done in a separate building like the one that contained this summer kitchen on Suydam's farm on Route 27. In winter, the cooking was brought back into the house, where the warmth it produced was welcome on cold days.

MIDDLEBUSH FARMER, *c.* 1935. Harold Wade is milking a Holstein, one of the top milk producers. The breed was brought to America by early Dutch settlers. Franklin farmers were once major grain producers. But after the Midwest opened up to settlement, wheat production moved westward. Franklin farmers lost the market for much of their grain, so many switched to raising cattle and dairy cows.

FROM FARM TO DAIRY, 1919. Milk from local farms was collected in 40-quart cans like the ones on this wagon. Farmers placed the cans on platforms alongside the road. A wagon then took them to a dairy such as Paulus Dairy in New Brunswick. This photograph shows the second Middlebush Reformed Church under construction.

PRIZE-WINNING SHEEP, 1904. John L. Suydam of Franklin Park had a winner with his Southdown buck. The Southdown is an English breed that produces high-quality meat. Sheep were often kept by Franklin farmers for meat and wool. Eventually, raising sheep became too expensive, even as a sideline.

JOHN VOORHEES FARM, PLEASANT PLAINS, 1904. Voorhees' array of barns and outbuildings was not unusual for that era. As farmers added new equipment or more animals, they needed more space, so they tacked another building onto the string.

FRANKLIN FARMHOUSES, 1904, 1905. The Griggstown farmhouse of Stephen Garretson (above) and the Pleasant Plains farmhouse of John Voorhees (below) are typical of those found in Franklin a century ago. The materials used to build early farmhouses depended on whatever natural resources were at hand. Franklin had abundant forests and many sawmills, so wooden farmhouses like these were common. The buildings were covered with a sheathing of clapboard or cedar shingles, or sometimes both. Paint was costly, so some frugal farmers would simply allow the wood to weather darken; others would just paint the front and sides that showed from the road. The back would remain unpainted.

SOMERSET FARM, *c*. 1910s. Udo Fleischmann raised and trained horses at Somerset Farm on the outskirts of East Millstone. His cousins operated the distillery in East Millstone from 1880 to 1910. When the original barn was destroyed by fire around 1906, Fleischmann built one of the first structured-concrete buildings in the United States. In 1919, he sold the farm to his brother-in-law, John Wyckoff Mettler, and moved to Florida. The land is now part of Colonial Park.

# *Two*
# The Canal and the Railroad

DELAWARE AND RARITAN CANAL AT ZAREPHATH, c. 1915.

CANAL-BOAT VIEW OF SWING BRIDGE, EAST MILLSTONE, c. 1909. When the Delaware and Raritan Canal opened in 1834, it was one of America's greatest artificial waterways. About 22 miles of the main canal ran along the western and northern borders of Franklin Township, parallel to the Millstone and Raritan Rivers.

MULES PULLING A COAL BARGE, EAST MILLSTONE, EARLY 1900s. In its heyday, the canal was a key transportation link between Philadelphia and New York, carrying the coal and other heavy materials that helped build nineteenth-century industrial America. The peak time for the canal was the five years after the Civil War ended.

BOAT-TURNING BASIN, EAST MILLSTONE, *c.* 1910. Railroads cut heavily into the canal trade, leaving the waterway with less and less to carry. By 1900, the D&R Canal stopped showing a profit. When the canal ceased operating in 1933, its future was uncertain. There was even talk of filling it in. The State of New Jersey took it over in 1936 as a potential water source.

CUTTING ICE ON THE CANAL, EAST MILLSTONE, *c.* 1908. Ice cutting was an important chore every winter after the canal shut down. The ice was cut into uniform-size blocks, piled onto wagons, and then stored with sawdust in icehouses, where it would last until the next winter. The Peter Eugene Nevius house is in the background.

ZAREPHATH CANAL BRIDGE, *c. 1920s.* When the Pillar of Fire religious community settled at Zarephath in 1906, the D&R Canal ran through their property, and the Pennsylvania Railroad owned the right-of-way. The community received permission to build a bridge across the canal to provide access to their property on the western side.

CUSTOMIZED CANAL BOAT, *c. 1920s.* The Pillar of Fire purchased a sailboat in 1911 to use on the canal. They removed the sail, reconditioned the boat, and installed an engine. A small wharf was built at the edge of the canal. The boat served the community until the 1930s.

LOCKING THROUGH, c. 1910s, 1920s. As the D&R Canal flowed through Franklin toward New Brunswick, water levels changed by almost 24 feet. From a high of 56.3 feet at Kingston, the water dropped to 48.8 feet at the Griggstown Lock (above) and 40.9 at the Ten Mile Lock near Zarephath (below). The next lock, at South Bound Brook, was 32.5 feet. The canal was open from April 1 to mid-December, weather permitting, but it closed on Sunday. The hours for *locking through*—moving from one water level to another through the locks—were usually from 6 am to 6 pm.

F.W. BRUNE, KINGSTON LOCKS, *c.* 1901. For some residents who lived near the locks, *locking through* was a source of endless fascination. They enjoyed watching as the boat entered the lock, the gates swung shut, and the vessel moved with the changing water level.

MULE TENDER'S BARRACKS, GRIGGSTOWN CAUSEWAY, EARLY 1900s. This building was used by canal construction workers and, later, mule tenders. Today, it houses a museum.

WATER SPORTS, *c.* 1910s. These two photographs of Griggstown show three favorite canal and river activities: fishing, swimming, and canoeing. In 1972, the D&R Canal Coalition—more than thirty environmental and historical groups who joined forces to preserve the canal—deluged the state with letters on behalf of the treasured waterway and pushed to have it declared a national historic site and a state park. The following year, the D&R Canal and canal-related structures were placed on the National and New Jersey Registers of Historic Places. The Delaware and Raritan Canal State Park was created in 1974. In 1992, the park's trail system was designated a National Recreation Trail.

GRISTMILL AT GRIGGSTOWN, c. 1900. Benjamin Griggs' mill was built in the 1730s. Activity at the mill in pre-Revolutionary times made it the center of the village that would take Griggs' name. In the 1830s, the mill was in the path of the canal. It was torn down and a new one (shown on the far left) was built next to the causeway.

LOVERS LANE, c. 1910s. Lovers Lane is really the Griggstown Causeway. It extends across a strip of land between the D&R Canal and the Millstone River and connects with a bridge across the river. It is now within the Delaware and Raritan Canal State Park.

BLACKWELLS MILLS, EARLY 1900s. These two photographs, taken at the same time, show the buildings on Canal Road at the Blackwells Mills Causeway. The 1980 D&R Canal historic survey identified fifteen historic houses in the Blackwells Mills district. Most are along Canal Road. A number of barns and outbuildings connected to eighteenth- and nineteenth-century farms are still standing. Blackwells Mills did not enjoy the economic prosperity the D&R Canal brought to some villages of Franklin.

BLACKWELLS MILLS BRIDGE-TENDER'S HOUSE, BUILT 1830s. When the D&R Canal closed in 1933, bridge tender Sandor Fekete was permitted to remain in this house. After he died in 1970, the building began to deteriorate. The Blackwells Mills Canal House Association came to the rescue. This photograph shows the restored structure that opened in 1972. The house is managed by The Meadows Foundation.

GRIGGSTOWN'S SWING BRIDGE, EARLY 1900s. Swing-type bridges along the waterway required the D&R Canal Company to provide bridge tenders. When a bell rang, the gate on the west bank would be closed. Then the tender opened the bridge that was balanced on sets of iron wheels that moved along a track on a turntable.

SWING BRIDGE, ROCKY HILL, c. 1906. The shed at the left of the bridge held the mechanism the bridge tender used to swing the structure aside for passing boats. Barney McCloskey's Tavern is in the center background.

SWING BRIDGE, EAST MILLSTONE, c. 1912. When kids heard the signal that the swing bridge was about to be moved, they would rush to hitch a ride on it. The canal offered an appealing contrast to everyday life in rural Franklin Township. Families who lived along the canal often sat on the banks in the summertime and watched the boats go by.

SWING BRIDGE, MAIN STREET, KINGSTON, EARLY 1900s. Groundbreaking for the D&R Canal was at Kingston in November 1830. Telegraph stations were maintained at several locations along the canal, including Kingston. The D&R Canal is believed to have occasioned the earliest commercial use of the Morse telegraph in the United States.

CANAL AND RAILROAD BUILDINGS, ROCKY HILL, EARLY 1900s. The canal bridge and bridge-tender's house were next to the Rocky Hill Railroad Station. The canal was important to Rocky Hill. Lumber came down the canal to a sawmill. Farmers used the canal to send their produce to New Brunswick.

MILLSTONE AND NEW BRUNSWICK RAILROAD, c. 1907. Until the 1850s, East Millstone was called Johnsville for major landowner John Wyckoff. The village's name was changed when a railroad was planned from New Brunswick to Flemington. In 1854, the Millstone and New Brunswick Railroad Company laid out 6 miles of single-lane track as far as East Millstone. It never extended beyond the canal or the Millstone River, but it did bring an economic boom to East Millstone. The picture of the East Millstone Railroad Station (above) and the view looking west toward East Millstone (below) were taken around the same time.

ACTION ON THE RAILROAD, *c.* 1910. The photograph of railroad workers (above) was taken near the train station in East Millstone. The snow picture (below) was taken in East Millstone in January 1910. To clear the tracks, the trains would plow the snow, stop, shovel it away, and then move forward. It was not unusual for younger male passengers to be issued shovels to help clear the path for the train to get through. A heavy snow could halt train service altogether.

ALL ABOARD, *c.* 1905. Baggage man William Wyckoff has his head out the door as conductor Oliver Swenson (foreground) signals "All Aboard." Chris Hockenbury is in the gray suit. One of the others near him is Mike Coyle. The railroad provided direct service to New York via Jersey City. This encouraged a number of New York businessmen to settle in the East Millstone area.

BOARDING THE TRAIN AT EAST MILLSTONE, 1906. The man's identity is not known. He ran errands for people in East Millstone. The Millstone and New Brunswick line had four train stations in Franklin: East Millstone, Middlebush, Clyde Road, and Voorhees (where the tracks crossed Route 27).

TRAIN ACCIDENTS, 1904, 1907. The 1904 accident (above) occurred near East Millstone. The 1907 train accident (below) was just over the border in New Brunswick, at the next stop beyond Voorhees Station. Passenger service on the Millstone and New Brunswick Railroad ended in 1930. After that, the track was used only occasionally for freight trains to the rubber reclaiming factory in East Millstone.

MIDDLEBUSH TRAIN STATION, *c.* 1906. The train gave villagers easy access to a large shopping area. The trip from Middlebush to downtown New Brunswick took less than twenty minutes. The convenient rail line attracted many people to Franklin.

BERTHA TOTTEN'S HOUSE, 1934. When John Thuman built this house in the 1880s, he anticipated great growth in the village of Middlebush that would necessitate a two-track rail line. He built the house on the north side of Railroad Avenue, expecting to convert it into a train station. It remained a private residence.

MIDDLEBUSH STATION, *c.* 1940s. This picture was taken shortly before the Middlebush Railroad Station was torn down in 1948. The 12-foot-by-24-foot structure was the last of the four Millstone and New Brunswick stations in Franklin to be demolished.

RAILROAD CROSSING, SOUTH MIDDLEBUSH ROAD, *c.* 1908. The tracks ran along the south end of Middlebush. The station was on the south side of Railroad Avenue between South Middlebush Road and Olcott Avenue.

WESTON STATION NEAR ZAREPHATH, *c.* 1910s. This rail line was built originally as the New York and Philadelphia Air Line and ran from North Plainfield to Hillsborough. Later, as part of the Pennsylvania and Reading Railroad, it extended into Pennsylvania. It was located just west of Franklin near Weston.

ROCKY HILL RAILROAD STATION, c. 1911. The station was situated more for the convenience of industry than passenger use. It was at the end of the village on the Franklin Township side of the Millstone River and the D&R Canal, away from most residents. The tracks extended to the nearby Atlantic Terra Cotta Company.

# *Three*
# Commerce and Industry

EAST MILLSTONE, c. 1910.

MARKET STREET, EAST MILLSTONE, 1905 (ABOVE); *c.* 1910 (BELOW). A small commercial center was established in the village in 1834, when the Delaware and Raritan Canal opened. Market Street was laid out parallel to the canal. East Millstone continued to prosper after the Millstone and New Brunswick Railroad opened in 1854. The village loosened its ties to Franklin Township in 1873 and became a separate town. In 1949, the state mandated that East Millstone either incorporate as a separate borough or return to the full jurisdiction of Franklin Township. For economic reasons the villagers voted to rejoin Franklin.

ODD FELLOWS HALL, *c.* 1912. This building on Market Street in East Millstone has been home to many businesses since it was constructed in the 1870s, including Thatcher's Drugstore, a bakery, and Fagan's harness shop. It became Odd Fellows Hall after the Millstone Lodge No. 254, I.O.O.F, was organized in 1898. In 1942, it was converted into Millstone Valley Fire Department's firehouse. Today, it is the post office.

CANAL STREET, *c.* 1910. This street once ran along the D&R Canal in East Millstone. In this picture, Pace's Hotel (also known as Rail Road Hotel) is in the foreground, at the corner of Canal Street and Livingston Avenue. The building with the cupola is a storehouse. The one next to it with the porch is Wilson's Store. The A-shaped canal swing bridge is visible at the left.

## HARMER RUBBER RECLAIMING WORKS
### EAST MILLSTONE, N. J.

HARMER RUBBER RECLAIMING WORKS, *c.* 1911. Fleischmann's distillery was the major industry in East Millstone for thirty years. When Fleischmann moved to New York in 1910, the factory was sold to Harmer Rubber Reclaiming Works. It has also operated as Somerset Rubber Company and Laurie Rubber Reclaiming Company. AGI Rubber Company bought the company in 1975 and operated it until 1983.

DEVASTATING FIRE, 1912. The rubber reclaiming factory was hit by a spectacular fire on October 28, 1912. A hastily formed fire brigade found the flames too intense to prevent them from spreading across Livingston Avenue to Pace's Hotel and Gerhart's house and store. Other houses on Market Street were also destroyed.

COOPER'S STORE, *c.* 1909. One of these three distinguished gentlemen standing in front of Cooper's Store in East Millstone is probably the owner, Thomas Cooper. This picture was the subject of a William W. Tetlow postcard. Tetlow took hundreds of photographs of East Millstone and its residents in the early twentieth century.

BENNETT'S GARAGE, EAST MILLSTONE, LATE 1920s. Bennett's was one of the earliest service stations on Amwell Road. The local bus line departed from there. Today, Onka's Charter Bus Service still leaves from there. Amwell Road was the first road in Franklin to be paved. It was macadamized in 1901.

MERRELL'S COZY NOOK. This early version of a convenience store was near the site of the present Millstone Valley Fire Department's firehouse on Amwell Road in East Millstone. Roadside stores such as Merrell's became popular when cars provided township residents greater mobility.

VAN LIEW FARMHOUSE, *c.* 1909. This historic building is perhaps the oldest structure in East Millstone. In June 1777, Lord Cornwallis is believed to have occupied it while the British and Americans engaged in a five-day standoff that determined the direction of the war. After the Delaware and Raritan Canal opened, it became the Franklin House. Today, as the Franklin Inn, it houses a used-book store administered by The Meadows Foundation.

EARLY GRIGGSTOWN STORE, *c.* 1910s. The old Griggstown Store opened for business before 1850, and carried a variety of merchandise. The store was bought by Harvey Boice after 1905 and operated with the help of Charles Cheston (in foreground, weighing a wagon). The building sustained heavy fire damage around 1921.

RECENT GRIGGSTOWN STORE, *c.* 1930s. Mr. and Mrs. Herman Kunze purchased several rental bungalows in 1927 and set up shop in one of the huts. The store and bungalows were sold in 1930 to Mr. and Mrs. Sigrud Berven. Edward and Rose Tornquist owned the store from 1942 to 1972, and then sold it to Michael and Florence Mason. It was eventually closed, and the building was converted into apartments.

TERRA COTTA INDUSTRY IN ROCKY HILL, *c.* 1920s. The Rocky Hill area had large clay deposits, a prime location on the D&R Canal, and was accessible to railroads. Excelsior Terra Cotta Company opened in 1894. In 1907, Excelsior joined with Atlantic Terra Cotta Company of New York and Perth Amboy Terra Cotta Company to form the Atlantic Terra Cotta conglomerate. It became the world's largest manufacturer of architectural terra cotta. High-quality terra cotta produced at Atlantic's Rocky Hill facility and other plants adorned many important structures, including the Woolworth Building in New York and the Philadelphia Art Museum.

DIMINISHED DEMAND. As the demand for architectural terra cotta declined, so did the factory's production. Downsizing led to the closing of the Rocky Hill plant around 1930. Atlantic went bankrupt in 1943. All the buildings shown here fell to ruins, with the exception of one that was later used as an artist's studio.

NORDENBROOK'S GENERAL STORE, c. 1910. Today, this building on Canal Road in Blackwells Mills is a bright red barn. In 1910, it was Nordenbrook's General Store and the Blackwells Mills Post Office. Before that, it was a blacksmith shop. Nordenbrook moved to the Franklin Township side of the river after his store in Hillsborough burned down.

COPPER MINING IN FRANKLIN TOWNSHIP, 1905. The copper mine between Rocky Hill and Griggstown enticed speculators and prospectors for almost two centuries with little success. Mining was first attempted in the early 1700s by John Stevens. These pictures were taken during a failed effort by the New Jersey Copper Company to work the mine in 1905. Shown are the following: (above) the shaft and boiler house; (below) investors standing near the mouth of the drainage tunnel. The last attempt to work the mine was in 1916. Today, the only vestige of Franklin's copper-mining past can be found in a street name: Copper Mine Road.

FRANKLIN'S TRAP ROCK QUARRY, *c.* 1900s. The quarry in southern Franklin has been in operation since before the 1850s and has had several names. During the 1860s, it produced paving block used to surface miles of streets in Jersey City and Newark. After the Civil War, it was Howell's Quarries. When these two photographs were taken, it was the Delaware River Quarry Company with 300 employees, including 250 Italian immigrants. As Kingston Trap Rock in the 1950s, it quarried rock used to construct the New Jersey Turnpike. Today, quarrying is carried on by Trap Rock Industries.

WESTON MILL, BUILT *c.* 1740s. The historic Weston Mill is only a memory now, but for almost 250 years it was an important part of Franklin's landscape. The mill was raided by the British searching for flour during the American Revolution. The mill passed through a series of owners until the 1920s, when Wilbur Smith purchased it. Over the years, Smith attempted to restore the building. In 1982, the structure collapsed into the Millstone River and was declared a flood hazard. Engineers determined it was irrevocably destroyed and would cost too much to rebuild, but the machinery and timbers were worth saving. In June 1983, a group of volunteers began removing the mill's contents.

TRACES OF THE PAST. Volunteers salvaged a cornerstone from 1844 (the year the mill was rebuilt) with the name of Cornell, who owned the mill at that time. They made plans to resume their recovery work on July 9, 1983. Early on the morning of the 9th, the remains of the historic Weston Mill went up in flames. Police later arrested two Manville teenagers for setting the fire.

JOHN SCHUESSLER'S GULF INN, 1924. Schuessler operated a gas station/food stand on Route 27 in the Kingston section of Franklin Township. He constructed this pavilion for local celebrations and dances.

HOFFMAN HOUSE HOTEL, KINGSTON, c. 1900. The hotel on Main Street later burned down. The house on the right was moved to another location. Kingston was an important stop for travelers from its earliest years. The King's Highway (Main Street/Route 27) was widened as early as 1701. Stagecoach drivers traveling between New York and Philadelphia often changed horses at Kingston.

KINGSTON HOTEL, c. 1930s. After the Hoffman House on Main Street was destroyed by fire, the Kingston Hotel went up in its place. Like its predecessor, the Kingston Hotel also burned down. The fire was in the early 1940s, during World War II.

LUTHER ANTHONY'S GENERAL STORE, KINGSTON, JULY 4, 1904. The store was at the corner of Laurel Avenue and Main Street (Route 27). Today, it is the Main Street Cafe.

KINGSTON BUILDINGS, MAIN STREET (ROUTE 27). Kingston Garden is on the left in this photograph. Vince Petrillo was the proprietor. Next door is the Garden Tonsorial Parlor (Armand Petrillo's Barber Shop). The Somerset County Magistrate's Office shares the other half of the building. Kingston Garden was torn down when Good Time Charlie's expanded. The small building on the right still stands.

KINGSTON POST OFFICE. At one time, the Kingston Post Office was in the building (above) that is now connected to Lou's Barber Shop on Main Street. Below, Raymond Woolf, postmaster of Kingston, sits behind the wheel of his car in front of 7 Laurel Avenue in 1942. One of Kingston's early post offices was at 64 Main Street; that building later became a grocery and, still later, an antiques store. Another post office was on the site of the old Post House Inn.

J.S. WOOLFE, BOOT AND SHOEMAKER. Woolfe's shop was on Main Street in Kingston. The building, now a private residence, stands next to Lou's Barber Shop.

LAIRD'S CORNER, PLEASANT PLAINS, EARLY 1900s. The earliest building at Laird's Corner dates back to about 1800 and was once a blacksmith shop. A general store was added in 1870. The Laird family arrived in 1878. The buildings are still standing at the intersection of South Middlebush and Suydam Roads, surrounded by K. Hovnanian's Town and Country Estates housing development.

BEEKMAN'S HOTEL, FRANKLIN PARK, 1904. Christopher Columbus Beekman built his hotel on land that had been occupied by taverns since colonial times. Gifford's Tavern was there during the American Revolution. From 1796 to 1868, the tavern was kept by Moore Baker and his son William. William Williamson ran it as the Franklin House from 1868 to 1874. The building was then torn down and Beekman's Hotel went up on the spot. That structure burned in December 1929.

MATCHBOOK COVER VIEW, FRANKLIN PARK GRILL, c. 1950s. The Dutch barn on the Beekman Hotel/Franklin House property survived the 1929 fire and was converted to a restaurant known as Franklin Park Inn. The structure became Franklin Park Grill in the 1940s and Chauncey's in 1986.

HULLFISH'S STORE, 1905. The store, located on the South Brunswick side of Route 27 in Franklin Park, was also the post office and a favorite meeting place for villagers. The interior photograph (below) shows Postmaster Charles C. Hullfish at his desk. Franklin's earliest post office was established in 1826 in Franklin Park, when the village was known as Six Mile Run. Sometimes the post office was on the Middlesex County side of Route 27; at other times it was on the Somerset side in Franklin, depending on who was postmaster.

FATHER AND SON, 1904. Wheelwright Peter S. DeHart (right) and his son John stand in the doorway of Peter's wheelwright shop at Three Mile Run. Three Mile Run lost its identity as a village when the Somerset section of Franklin Township crowded in around it in the years after World War I.

HOME AND WHEELWRIGHT SHOP OF PETER S. DEHART, 1904. As long as people depended on wagons and carriages for transportation, they needed the services of wheelwrights like DeHart to make and repair their vehicles and wheels. Within a few years after this picture was taken, the impact of automobiles began to be felt. New jobs tied to automobile services soon replaced those of the wheelwright and blacksmith.

THE LAST BLACKSMITH, 1933. Joseph Roach was the last of Franklin's village blacksmiths. He worked in Millstone before moving to Middlebush in 1902 to set up his own shop. He retired in 1950 and died in 1954. Roach was Franklin's truant officer for many years and served as a juror for the Hall-Mills murder trial in 1926. His shop on the corner of Smith Road and Olcott Avenue was torn down in 1956.

VOORHEES HOUSE, BUILT 1793. This fine old building on Amwell Road near DeMott Lane is the oldest house in Middlebush. It was built by Garret Voorhees Jr. in 1793 with money received from the government in compensation for the burning of an earlier house during the American Revolution. In 1834, the Middlebush Reformed Church was organized in the house. The Van Middlesworth family acquired the property in the late 1800s from the Voorhees family. When Mr. and Mrs. John Van Middlesworth opened Colonial Farms restaurant in 1939, it became a popular dining place. They operated it until 1971. O'Connor's of Watchung, New Jersey, reopened the restaurant in 1976. It remains today one of Franklin's favorite dining spots.

DOWNTOWN MIDDLEBUSH, *c.* 1905. Abram V.D. Stryker's wheelwright shop, center, did more than repair wagons and make wheels. Stryker built fine carriages known as "buggies." His building was torn down in 1923 and the lumber was used to build a private residence. The recycling of wood and even entire wooden structures was commonplace in Franklin. Nothing was wasted.

MIDDLEBUSH STORE AND POST OFFICE, BUILT *c.* 1854. This store, conveniently located near the Middlebush station, opened soon after the trains began running in 1854. It had several owners before John Smith purchased it in 1900. His son Elmer T. took over in 1909 and operated the store until 1945, when it was purchased by Nevin W. Kline.

AIR WAVES. Franklin Township has four radio stations: Zarephath is the home of WAWZ 1380 AM and WAWZ 99.1 FM, and Veronica Avenue is the home of WCTC 1450 AM and WMGQ 98.3 FM. WAWZ-AM began transmitting in 1931; it added an FM station in 1950. WCTC, which began transmitting from New Brunswick in 1946, relocated to Franklin in 1978. Above, New Brunswick students visit the station at Zarephath in 1938. Below, an aerial view of the Veronica Avenue facility shows the 505-foot tower soon after it was raised.

MAIN ROOM, MARCONI WIRELESS TELEGRAPH STATION, *c.* 1918. The Marconi Wireless Telegraph Station was built on Easton Avenue in 1911–13. In 1918, two of the most important messages of World War I were transmitted to the world from Franklin Township: Woodrow Wilson's historic Fourteen Points and his appeal for the abdication or overthrow of Kaiser Wilhelm II.

MARCONI STATION DURING WORLD WAR II. By the 1950s, technology at the station was obsolete. RCA removed its transmitting equipment in 1955 and took down the antennae. In 1992, Guglielmo Marconi Memorial Plaza was dedicated across the street. Marconi's daughter Gloria Marconi-Braga attended the ceremony.

HISTORIC VISIT, 1921. When David Sarnoff conducted an inspection tour in 1921, the Marconi Wireless Telegraph Station on Easton Avenue had become the RCA Transoceanic Station. This historic photograph of the tour visitors captured the images some of the greatest scientists of that time. Unfortunately, it didn't capture all their names. From left to right are three unidentified men, David Sarnoff, Thomas J. Hayden, Ernst Julius Berg, S. Benedict, Albert Einstein, Nicola Tesla, Charles Proteus Steinmetz, A.N. Goldsmith, A. Malsin, Irving Langmuir, Albert W. Hull, E.B. Pillsbury, Saul Dushman, Richard Howland Ranger, George Ashley Campbell, and two unidentified men. The man standing between Einstein and Steinmetz was originally identified as John Carson but later correctly identified as Nicola Tesla. One of the unknowns is believed to be Ernst Alexanderson.

# *Four*

# Serving the Community

FRANKLIN CONSTABLE CARL J. TREPTOW, LATE 1920s.

# LOOK !      LOOK !

## $100 REWARD

## The Aid and Detective Society of Franklin Park having learned that a number of its members have suffered loss by theft of their Poultry, and

WHEREAS, It is the purpose of the society to protect its members from loss and if there be a loss to do all in its power to punish the offender or offenders. Therefore be it

RESOLVED, That we offer a reward of $100.00 ($50.00 by the Aid and Detective Society of Franklin Park and $50.00 by the Consolidated Society of New Jersey and Pennsylvania) for the arrest and conviction of the thief or thieves.

### MEMBERS

| | | | |
|---|---|---|---|
| MRS. ANNIE H. STANEK | MABUS BROS. | MATTHEW SUYDAM | J. G. CORTELYOU |
| CONRAD ICKE | G. V. SUYDAM | FRANK G. HART | J. V. GARRETSON |
| MRS. J. A. BODINE | HENRY RULE, EST. | H. B. SKILLMAN | VAN DYKE HIGGINS |
| MRS. B. S. GRIGGS | WILLIAM WYCKOFF | L. S. LYDECKER | WILLIAM J. CORTELYOU |
| WILLIAM BRUECHNER | JACOB FRITZ | PETER CORTELYOU | IRVING HOAGLAND |
| REV. E. H. KEATOR | T. E. GIBSON | MRS. ELIZABETH C. GARRETSON | WALTER HUTCHINSON |
| MRS. GARRETSON HAGEMAN | MISS MARY NEVIUS | HANS MAUCHES | F. M. BODINE |
| A. S. VOORHEES | DR. J. C. DUNN | ASA HIGGINS | MRS. J. A. VOORHEES |
| W. V. GIBSON | A. V. D. POLHEMUS, EST. | H. A. LANGBEIN | PETER C. S. HAGEMAN |
| | | A. W. TOTTEN | |

**T. E. GIBSON, President**

**J. G. CORTELYOU, Secretary**

EARLY CRIME FIGHTERS. The Aid and Detective Society of Franklin Park was organized in 1878. When members learned of a theft, they sprang into action. If they caught the thief, they turned the culprit over to the law for trial. Like the other vigilante groups in the township at the time, the Franklin Park crime fighters were never paid for their efforts. They disbanded in 1940, the year the Franklin Township Police Department was officially established.

SURVEYING THE CRIME SCENE, 1935. Constable Bruno J. Miller appears at the site of the Hall-Mills murders. Thirteen years earlier, the bodies of Reverend Edward Wheeler Hall, forty-one-year-old rector of a New Brunswick church, and Mrs. Eleanor Mills, his thirty-four-year-old choir singer/lover, were found side-by-side near a crabapple tree on the abandoned Phillips Farm in Franklin Township. Houses in the background show that by 1935, the once-secluded area was beginning to be built up.

DERUSSEY LANE CRIME SCENE, 1922. The Hall-Mills murders dominated the news for months in the 1920s. More was written about them than any other murder to that point in U.S. history. The murder scene was a magnet for curious followers of the story. Crowds trampled the area for souvenirs. After the crime-scene tree (above) was stripped bare, entrepreneurs removed bark from other trees and sold it as the real thing.

GIBSON'S HOME, 1922. Franklin pig farmer Jane Gibson said she saw Hall's wife and brother-in-law at the crime scene the night of the Hall-Mills murders. Gibson, dubbed the "Pig Woman" by the press, lived in this building near the Hamilton Avenue end of DeRussey Lane. Despite her claim, there was not enough evidence to indict. Four years later, new allegations surfaced; in 1926, Hall's widow, her brothers, and a cousin were arrested and indicted. All four were acquitted.

CONSTABLE BRUNO J. MILLER, c. 1940. Franklin Township's twelve constables formed a volunteer police organization in 1933 and petitioned to be known as the Franklin Township Police Department. The application was accompanied by a release absolving the township of liability but was nonetheless rejected by the township committee. The group continued to act as a volunteer police organization until 1940.

FIRST PATROL CAR, 1942. Chief Edwin F. Voorhees stands next to the Franklin Township Police Department's first patrol car. The department was officially established in 1940 with the enactment of the police ordinance. Voorhees was named the first chief. He held that post until he retired in 1958.

RUSSELL N. PFEIFFER, 1947. Franklin had a part-time police department until 1953. Members held other full-time jobs to support themselves and their families. Pfeiffer was named police lieutenant in January 1953 and became Franklin Township's first full-time officer. He succeeded Edwin F. Voorhees as chief of the department in 1958 and retired in 1978, after thirty-three years of service.

10TH ANNIVERSARY, 1950. The Franklin Township Police Department had grown to twelve members when this 10th anniversary photograph was taken in 1950. From left to right are (front row) Lieutenant Douglas Woitcheck, Chief Edwin F. Voorhees, and Police Commissioner Russell Laird; (middle row) Russell Pfeiffer, Naaman Williams, Albert Bessenyei, Charles Petrillo, and William Ribar; (back row) George Newell, Louis Schunk, Adolph Canavesio, and Thomas J. Lee.

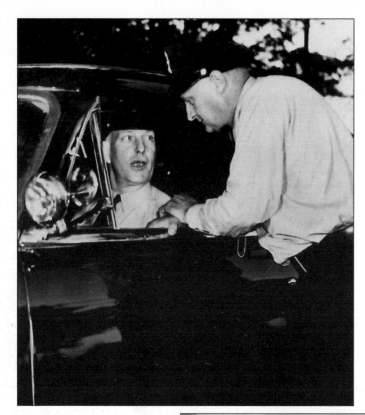

FIRST SERGEANT. The position of sergeant was created in the Franklin Township Police Department in 1956. The new post went to Adolph Canavesio (right), who is talking with Patrolman Thomas Lee in this 1952 photograph. In 1933, Canavesio was a member of the police volunteer group that sought to establish a police department.

RADIO LINK, 1960. The Franklin Township Police Department's first radio communication system was installed in 1954 and hailed as a complete success. It was on the same wavelength as those of departments in surrounding townships, which made cooperation easier. This photograph shows Sergeant James Brown at police headquarters in Middlebush. The department moved to the new municipal building on DeMott Lane in 1972.

FRANKLIN'S FINEST, 1958. From left to right are (front row) Charles Spangenberg, Naaman Williams, Chief Russell Pfeiffer, L. Collier, and Matthew J. Miller; (back row) James Brown, W. Ciampra, John Lebed, C. Paul, George W. Dunham, William Ribar, and Edward Nelson. Patrolman Miller was forty when he died suddenly of a heart attack a year after this picture was taken. A year later, on July 10, 1960, the department suffered a double tragedy. Patrolmen Lebed and Dunham were killed in the line of duty.

EARLY FIREFIGHTER. The Middlebush Volunteer Fire Department is the oldest of the ten volunteer companies that serve Franklin Township. It was founded in 1916, after a devastating fire destroyed five barns and threatened the village of Middlebush. Shortly after the department organized, members purchased this hand-drawn chemical apparatus. It would be their fire-fighting apparatus for many years.

DRAYTON'S GONG. In 1916, J. Morrison Drayton procured the rim of an old locomotive driving wheel and suspended it from a tree as Middlebush Volunteer Fire Department's first fire alarm. The alarm was sounded by hitting the wheel like a gong with a sledgehammer. When the department moved to Olcott Avenue, Drayton's gong was placed in front of the new firehouse as a reminder of the earlier years.

SIMPLEX ENGINE, 1938. This engine, purchased in 1927, was the Middlebush Volunteer Fire Company's first truck. The first firehouse was completed on DeBow Street in 1928. The company received its charter in 1929. Financial support in these early years came from donations, dues, suppers, and dances. The driver in this Independence Day parade photograph is Russell Totten.

LADIES AID, EARLY 1940s. The Ladies' Auxiliary of the Middlebush Volunteer Fire Department was organized in October 1941. Through sales, card parties, dances, suppers, a play, and other fund-raisers, they furnished the firehouse, provided equipment and uniforms, and placed a monument in front of the firehouse. They are shown here marching in an Independence Day parade.

KINGSTON VOLUNTEER FIRE COMPANY. The second oldest of the ten companies that serve Franklin Township was established in 1924. As in the case of the other companies, the impetus for its founding was a serious fire. A building between Laurel Avenue and the Kingston Presbyterian Church caught fire. The fire spread to an adjoining building and raised the concern of Kingston residents. The company's firehouse on Heathcote Road in South Brunswick was completed in the 1930s.

LENDING A HELPING HAND, MID-1950s. Mrs. Julia Yuras and daughter Linda of Little Rocky Hill assist Fire Chief Charles Petrillo in providing water to Kingston during a water shortage. Petrillo was the first of Franklin Township's special police in the early 1930s. He served as fire chief of the Kingston Volunteer Fire Department for five years.

MILLSTONE VALLEY FIRE DEPARTMENT. Franklin's third fire company was established in 1929. The group took over the Odd Fellows Hall on Market Street in East Millstone and converted it to a firehouse in 1942 (see p. 45). The third floor was removed during the renovations. The department moved to its present firehouse on Amwell Road in 1977.

FRANKLIN'S ROAD DEPARTMENT, *c.* 1939. From left to right are Sammy Smith, Fred Bascom, and unknown. One of the earliest powers given by the state to municipalities was the authority to build and maintain roads. Franklin has had surveyors and overseers of its highways since the township was incorporated in 1798.

FIRST MUNICIPAL BUILDING, BUILT 1916. Franklin Township's first town hall was at the corner of Amwell Road and Olcott Avenue. The building was constructed as Middlebush School No. 6, on the same site as Schoolhouse No. 5. The structure was used for classes until 1926. It then served as Franklin's town hall for almost a half century. The new municipal building on DeMott Lane opened in 1972.

FRANKLIN'S FIRST PUBLIC LIBRARY, c. 1958. The Madeline E. Lazar Memorial Library began in 1958 in a basement room of the Pine Grove Cooperative Apartments, adjacent to the Pine Grove School. The Lazar Library closed in 1964, and Franklin Township Public Library opened on Hamilton Street. The library moved to its present location on DeMott Lane in 1980.

# Five

# Places to Worship, Places to Learn

SIX MILE RUN REFORMED CHURCH, FRANKLIN PARK, 1817–1879.

SIX MILE RUN REFORMED CHURCH, 1766–1817. A Dutch Reformed congregation was established in Franklin in 1710. The first church was built along the Old Road (Route 27) before 1745. In 1766, a new church was built at Six Mile Run. During the American Revolution, a British soldier stood on the steps of Gifford's Tavern and shot a musket ball through the church weathervane. This church was replaced in 1817 by one that stood until 1879.

FRELINGHUYSEN MEMORIAL CHAPEL, 1911. After a fire destroyed the Six Mile Run Reformed Church in 1879, the congregation immediately began to build a new one. It was dedicated later that year. The chapel, shown here, was completed in 1907 and dedicated the following year.

MIDDLEBUSH REFORMED CHURCH, FOUNDED 1834. Before the church was established, local residents worshiped in Hillsborough, Six Mile Run, and New Brunswick. In 1835, this white frame church was completed on the corner of Amwell and South Middlebush Roads. The building was struck by lightning on July 2, 1917, and burned to the ground.

SECOND MIDDLEBUSH REFORMED CHURCH. Soon after the first church was destroyed by fire in 1917, the congregation began planning a new building on the same site. Construction was delayed by World War I. The dedication was held in 1919. Stone for the Tudor Gothic church came from quarries in Martinsville, New Jersey.

REFORMED CHURCH, EAST MILLSTONE, c. 1910. The building used since 1975 by the Calvary Baptist Church on Franklin Street was constructed in 1855 as a Dutch Reformed church. The building is typical of the Greek Revival style that was popular for church architecture in the mid-nineteenth century.

DON'T LOOK DOWN, 1909. East Millstone photographer William W. Tetlow took this picture of young Jack Garretson painting the steeple of the East Millstone Dutch Reformed Church.

ST. JOSEPH'S ROMAN CATHOLIC CHURCH, *c.* 1910. Father Bernard McArdle, pastor of St. Peter's Roman Catholic Church in New Brunswick, said Mass in 1832 in a house near Blackwells Mills for Irish families living in the Millstone area. In 1851, Father John Rodgers, also of St. Peter's, celebrated Mass in East Millstone homes. St. Joseph's was built on Livingston Avenue in East Millstone in 1865.

UNITED METHODIST CHURCH, *c.* 1910. Andrew Vroom and some members of the Methodist church congregation in Hillsborough were vehemently opposed to slavery. They parted company with the Hillsborough church and built this one in 1854 on Elm Street in East Millstone, where they could make known their abolitionist views.

PILLAR OF FIRE CHURCH AUDITORIUM, BUILT 1918. In 1906, Alma White's Pentecostal Union religious community moved to the Garretson farm in northwest Franklin and renamed it Zarephath. The Pentecostal Union's name was changed in 1917 to Pillar of Fire.

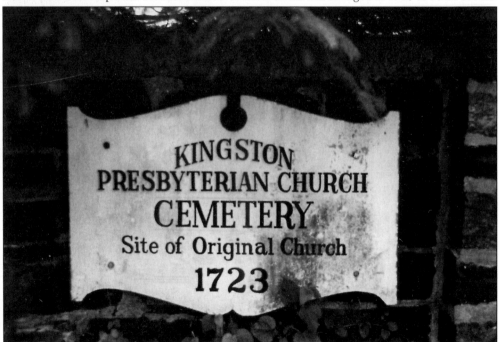

FATEFUL DECISION. After battles at Trenton and Princeton, Washington and his war-weary army marched to Kingston. On January 3, 1777, he and his officers held a conference on horseback atop a hill near the Presbyterian church. When they saw the British advance guard approaching, they decided not to try to capture New Brunswick. Instead, Washington took his troops north of the Raritan for the winter.

GRIGGSTOWN REFORMED CHURCH, c. 1910. The building is a superb example of mid-nineteenth-century Greek Revival architecture: it has a temple front with a recessed entry porch, two Doric columns, and four pilasters. A belfry with pilasters and dentil cornices top the building. The Griggstown Reformed Church, built in 1842, is one of the oldest continuously occupied churches in the area.

FRANKLIN'S FIRST SYNAGOGUE. Members of the Jewish poultry farming community all contributed to build this small white frame structure on Davidson Avenue in the 1930s. Newer Jewish residents reorganized in 1963 as Temple Beth El of Somerset. The Davidson Avenue temple was not adequate to meet the needs of the expanding congregation. Temple Beth El on Amwell Road was dedicated in 1967.

STUDENTS, RARITAN RIVER SCHOOLHOUSE, 1913. The schoolhouse was on the south side of Easton Avenue, midway between DeMott Lane and Leupp Lane (JFK Boulevard). It was abandoned as a school in 1917. The building was torn down in the 1970s. Garden apartments are on the site today.

SOUTH MIDDLEBUSH SCHOOLHOUSE, BUILT c. 1858. This school on the southeast corner of South Middlebush Road and Skillmans Lane was abandoned in 1924. The building was later purchased by the Franklin Park Volunteer Fire Company, who moved it to Franklin Park on Route 27. In 1946, it was destroyed by fire.

MIDDLEBUSH SCHOOLHOUSE NO. 5, BUILT 1859. The school stood originally in back of the Reformed church. The second floor was used for Sunday school and prayer meetings. In 1907, the four upper grades were moved upstairs, making it Franklin's first two-room schoolhouse. In 1916, the building was moved across the street and used as a private residence. It was torn down around 1920.

OLDER STUDENTS, MIDDLEBUSH SCHOOLHOUSE NO. 5, c. 1910. Before 1871, free education was only for paupers; others had to pay tuition to attend public schools. Schools were made entirely tuition-free in 1871, when New Jersey provided for a school tax on property. State laws in 1913 and 1914 made education compulsory.

STUDENTS, EAST MILLSTONE SCHOOLHOUSE, *c.* 1909. From left to right are (front row) unknown, Delver Runyon, Frank Jonas, May Madison, Henrietta Meyers, Anna Madison, Maggie Jonas, Susan Mortimer, Harry Grouser, and Walter Ohm; (middle row) Ethel Runyon, Ruth Marino, Sophia Jonas, Evelyn Jones, Anna Waterhouse, Ethel Hemming, Winnie Meagher, Dorothy Runyon, Josephine Jonas, Magdalina Meyers, ? Young, and Gertrude Sanderson; (back row) Mr. Gillingham, Martin Metz, Russell Van Dorn, John Meagher, George Meyers, Harry Beggin, Wilbur Remsen, George Van Nuys, Julian Nevius, Herbert Ohm, Dudley Carl, and Paul Gilliland.

SPECIAL OCCASION, *c.* 1912. Girls in white dresses. Boys in best suits. The way these East Millstone school children are decked out in their Sunday clothes tells us this flag-raising ceremony was a special occasion.

INTERIOR OF A FRANKLIN TOWNSHIP SCHOOLHOUSE, EARLY 1900s. Franklin Township's early schools were exclusively one-room structures. Many were still being used in the early twentieth century. The schools were located approximately 3 miles apart—the distance a school child could be expected to walk or ride a horse each day.

GRIGGSTOWN SCHOOLHOUSE, BUILT 1849. The school was originally on Canal Road, just north of the Griggstown Reformed Church. In 1854, the church moved the building to land it owned nearby. Classes were held there until 1932. The building was moved again in 1960, behind the new church hall. The Griggstown Historical Society has restored the building as a schoolhouse.

SUNDAY SCHOOL PICNIC, 1906. Upper Ten Mile Run School was on Old Georgetown Road near Copper Mine Road. Woodlawn School, on Route 27 near Bunker Hill Road, was also known as Lower Ten Mile Run School.

STUDENTS, PLEASANT PLAINS SCHOOLHOUSE, 1912. Pleasant Plains Schoolhouse was originally on Suydam Road, about one-half mile from South Middlebush Road. It closed in 1930. When the school faced demolition, the Friends of the Pleasant Plains School was organized. The building was moved to a location behind the municipal complex in 1996.

DONKEY BUS. In 1911, the Franklin Township School Board awarded the first bus contract to Van Dyke Higgins to transport six pupils from the Franklin Park area to New Brunswick for high school. High school students attended classes outside the township until 1961, when Franklin High School opened.

MAUDE CARTER'S PRIVATE SCHOOL, EARLY 1900s. Carter operated a boarding school on Elm Street in East Millstone at the beginning of the twentieth century. The school was in a large brick house constructed around 1855. The building, known as the A.T. Vroom house, is one of several excellent examples of Italianate architecture found in the village.

KINDERGARTEN, 1949. Helen F. Mettler operated a free kindergarten on Welsh's Lane in East Millstone. When this picture was taken, the teacher was Ellen Francke. Robert S. Mettler is in the back row, second from the right. He served as a member of the township council for twenty years and was mayor of Franklin.

RUTGERS PREP CADET, c. 1903. Thomas Holcombe Mettler of East Millstone is wearing the Rutgers Preparatory School cadet uniform. Rutgers Prep, which was founded in 1766, was originally located in Franklin Township. When the county line was redrawn in 1850, Franklin lost the Rutgers campus. Today, Rutgers Prep is back in Franklin. It relocated from New Brunswick in 1959 to the 35-acre Wells estate on Easton Avenue.

# *Six*
# Highways and Byways

A COUNTRY ROAD IN FRANKLIN, *c.* 1910.

FRANKLIN PARK, 1905. Route 27 has had several names, including Kings Highway and Old Stage Road. It was the main stagecoach route between New York and Philadelphia. This photograph shows it as a rain-drenched, muddy road, but that would soon change. In 1913, the road was designated part of the Lincoln Highway and once again became a major artery—this time for automobiles.

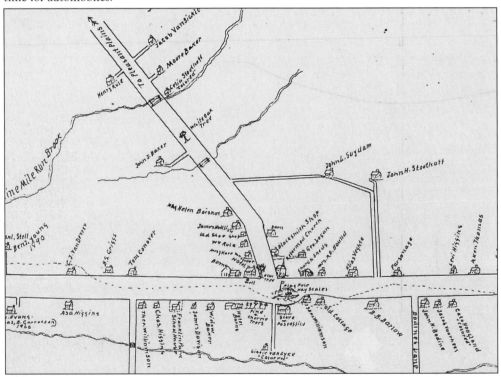

FRANKLIN PARK, 1893. After the first Somerset County Courthouse was built, Six Mile Run (Franklin Park) was a hub of county activity for almost a quarter century. When the courthouse burned in 1737, the county seat was moved to Millstone. Franklin Park resident Martin S. Garretson drew this map of his village in 1893. The dotted line shows the former route of the road that is now Route 27.

NEAR LANDING LANE BRIDGE, c. 1909. William W. Tetlow of East Millstone took this postcard picture of the road to Landing Lane Bridge near New Brunswick. Tetlow's postcards were popular among local residents who used them to correspond with others who were temporarily out of town or who had moved away from the village.

EAST MILLSTONE'S FIRST AUTOMOBILE, c. 1907. Charles Van Nostrand had the first automobile in East Millstone—a Stanley Steamer. Here, he is driving George Pace along Market Street. Pace, a lawyer, served in the New Jersey Assembly and owned Pace's Hotel. Pace lost his house, hotel, and office in devastating village fires.

IRON BRIDGE ACROSS THE MILLSTONE RIVER, BUILT 1901. The bridge, which connected East Millstone with Millstone, replaced an earlier wooden structure. The iron bridge was used until 1930. By then, automobile traffic had increased so much that a new bridge was needed. The new span was constructed several hundred feet south of this one.

UNFINISHED BRIDGE, c. 1907. H.F. Siebert of East Millstone published this picture postcard of the Millstone River at East Millstone, using a German chromolithograph process. The stone pillar was to have been part of the trestle bridge for the Millstone and New Brunswick Railroad, but the bridge was not completed when plans were canceled to extend the railroad beyond East Millstone.

THE BOARDWALK, 1903, 1909. A footbridge known as the Boardwalk once spanned the Millstone River and meadow from East Millstone to the town of Millstone. The 1909 picture (above) shows the wooden walkway that people used when the river was high or when snow was very deep. The earlier picture (below) was taken during a flood in August 1903.

WOODED WONDERLAND, *c.* 1910. These stately trees are part of perhaps the finest primeval forest in the eastern United States. John Wyckoff once owned this land in East Millstone. The forest has been known as Wyckoff's Woods, Howell's Woods, and Mettler's Woods. Today, as the William L. Hutcheson Memorial Forest, it is owned and managed by Rutgers University.

HISTORIC HIGHWAY, EARLY 1900s. Amwell Road is one of Franklin's most historic thoroughfares. It played a prominent role in the American Revolution. Several houses were destroyed or damaged by the British as they traveled the road to New Brunswick in 1777. Simcoe's Rangers used the road in 1779 after burning the county courthouse in Millstone.

INTERSECTION OF AMWELL AND SOUTH MIDDLEBUSH ROADS, 1935. Ten years earlier, the Middlebush Reformed Church granted the county the right to 18 feet or less of the northeast corner of its land to widen the road.

OLCOTT AVENUE, MIDDLEBUSH, 1908. Those utility poles were holding up telephone lines. The village was not wired for electricity until the 1920s. Middlebush was one of the first areas of Franklin to receive telephone service, a few years before this picture was taken.

ZAREPHATH DRIVE, c. 1920s. The Pillar of Fire imported four hundred blue spruce trees from Holland to beautify the Zarephath grounds. This photograph shows the trees lining the drive leading to the church auditorium. The Great Appalachian Storm that did heavy damage in Franklin in November 1950 produced some of the strongest winds ever to hit New Jersey. Many of the trees fell that day.

SUSPENDED WALKWAY, EARLY 1900s. A suspension bridge connected parts of the village of Rocky Hill in the days before automobiles. A boardwalk crossed the meadow, and a floating barrel bridge crossed the canal. A larger stone bridge spanned the Millstone River; another bridge crossed the canal on higher ground.

PLEASANT PLAINS, EARLY 1900s. Pleasant Plains had no defined boundaries. It was west of Franklin Park, south of Middlebush, and north of Ten Mile Run. The name was derived from the pleasantness of the surrounding lands—acres of gently rolling fields, farms, and hedgerows as far as the eye could see.

FRANKLIN TOWNSHIP SECTION OF KINGSTON, *c.* 1901. Historically, three villages stood at the midpoint between New York and Philadelphia, all with royal names: Princeton, Queenston, and Kingston. Two survive: Princeton and Kingston.

KINGSTON, WHERE THREE COUNTIES MEET: SOMERSET, MIDDLESEX, AND MERCER, 1884. Kingston also straddles three municipalities. The southernmost tip is in Franklin Township and Somerset County. The largest portion of Kingston is in South Brunswick and Middlesex County. The Princeton part of Kingston is in Mercer County. This nineteenth-century picture shows the crossroads: at right is the road to Princeton; in the center is the road to Rocky Hill/Franklin Township; and in the foreground is Kingston Bridge/South Brunswick.

# Seven
# The People of Franklin

OUT FOR A SPIN IN EAST MILLSTONE, *c.* 1910.

FRANKLIN TOWNSHIP'S NAMESAKE? William Franklin, the son of Benjamin Franklin, was New Jersey's last royal governor (1762–1776). Some historians are convinced that Franklin Township was named for William Franklin. Others argue for Benjamin. Not one document exists to identify the township's namesake conclusively, but there are strong arguments for both Franklins.

CAMPAIGNING IN EAST MILLSTONE. John Franklin Fort—hatless, facing the crowd—was governor of New Jersey from 1908 to 1911. Fort was the first politician in New Jersey to use the automobile cavalcade during his campaign. The building in the background is now gone. It stood across from the Franklin Inn.

EAST MILLSTONE BASEBALL TEAM, c. 1906. From left to right are (front row) George Barkalow, Frank Remsen, and unknown; (back row) Arthur Van Cleef, Charles Higgins, Lewis Welsh, unknown, and George Metz. The youngster in the foreground is Willie, Remsen's "bound boy." Bound boys, usually orphans, were placed in foster-type farm homes by the state. They attended school in winter and worked on the farm during the growing season.

ZAREPHATH LADIES AT THE POST OFFICE, c. 1910s. Pillar of Fire at Zarephath had a thriving publishing business. But the task of taking wagonloads of books and periodicals to the Bound Brook Post Office was so great that the community petitioned to have their own post office. Permission was granted, and the Zarephath Post Office opened in 1913.

WEDDING DAY IN EAST MILLSTONE, 1905. While Peter and Sadie were busy tying the knot inside the church in October 1905, others were busy outside tying signs, cans, and old shoes to the carriage (above). Family portraits were and are an important part of wedding receptions. This group (below) got together on the porch of an East Millstone house that October afternoon after Peter and Sadie were married.

NINETEENTH-CENTURY FAMILIES. Above, Allan Hooper, his wife Jane, and son Arthur are shown on their Franklin Park farm in 1896. Below, members of an unidentified Griggstown family sit in front of their home on Canal Road in Griggstown, c. 1890s. African-Americans have been a part of Franklin since the very early 1700s. An 1825 Franklin tax list indicates that thirty-six black men were property owners—at a time in U.S. history when many African-Americans elsewhere were enslaved and denied the right to own land.

CIVIL WAR SOLDIER. Nelson Wyckoff's name suggests his family members may have been slaves of the Wyckoffs, who were among Franklin Township's many slave owners. Black slavery in New Jersey began in 1680. Colonial Somerset County had New Jersey's second highest black population. The state's first legislative act to abolish slavery was in 1821. The practice wasn't abolished completely in New Jersey until 1846.

WAITING FOR THE SIGNAL, c. 1919. The three runners are on their mark and ready to race at a Boy Scout camp in Griggstown. Griggstown's beautiful scenery along the Delaware and Raritan Canal and the Millstone River has made it a popular location for such campsites. The round horn on the stand in back of the runners is part of a Victrola, an early phonograph player.

A LAZY SUMMER DAY IN FRANKLIN. Elton H.L. Wade of Middlebush took this picture of his nephews—George, Alan, and E. Leslie Wade—on the banks of the Millstone River for an Eastman Kodak international photograph contest. It won first prize for New Jersey and $100 for Wade. The photograph was used in a full-page ad on the back cover of the *Saturday Evening Post* on July 2, 1932.

INDEPENDENCE DAY IN MIDDLEBUSH, 1939, 1940. The day began with a parade of floats, fire trucks, bikes, and trikes that marched to the Middlebush Reformed Church. Cookies, lemonade, and peanuts were served while prizes were awarded. People then drifted home and waited to hear Drayton's gong signal the beginning of ball games that afternoon. In the evening, young and old played games on the church lawn. Firemen and Boy Scouts entertained with comic skits. Ice cream, cake, and lemonade rounded out the program.

GENTLE GIANT. The Middlebush Giant, whose stage name was Colonel Routh Goshen, was billed by P.T. Barnum as the tallest man in the world at 7 feet, 11 inches and 620 pounds. His true height was closer to 7 feet, 5 inches, and his weight during the Barnum years was about 400 pounds. Goshen spent many years in show business and lived about fifteen years in Middlebush, where he died in February 1889. Many mysteries surround Goshen, including his real name, age, and birthplace. A letter to the Middlebush Reformed Church in 1980 identified him as Arthur Caley, born in Sulby Village, Isle of Man, in 1827. Local residents remembered Goshen as a courteous, friendly neighbor with a great sense of humor. Circus folks and townspeople were frequent callers at his home on Amwell Road.

COMMAND PERFORMANCE.
Frances Sylvester of Middlebush was the
adopted daughter of the Middlebush
Giant. As a child, she traveled in
Germany and England and danced
before Great Britain's Queen Victoria.
Mrs. Sylvester died in 1949.

LOUISE FLEISCHMANN, c. 1900. The Fleischmann
family operated the distillery in East Millstone. Louise
was the sister of Udo Fleischmann and Helen
Fleischmann Mettler. She married Alfred B. McClay,
a noted horseman for whom the McClay Class—a
horse-show category—is named. She created the
McClay Gardens in Tallahassee, now owned by the
State of Florida.

LEWIS T. HOWELL FAMILY, *c.* 1857. Howell and his wife Joanna Maria Wyckoff are shown here with their two daughters, Gertrude and Sarah. Joanna was a descendant of John Wyckoff, for whom the village of Johnsville—now East Millstone—was named. Gertrude married William E. Mettler. Sarah married Howard DeMott.

JOHN WYCKOFF METTLER, *c.* 1930s. Mettler, of East Millstone, was founder and president of the Interwoven Stocking Company, the largest men's hosiery company in the world. He was an active alumnus of Rutgers and served on the board of trustees for many years. Mettler Hall, a Rutgers residence hall, is named in his honor.

VOTE FOR

# PETER C. S. HAGEMA]

REPUBLICAN CANDIDATE

## FOR TAX COLLECTO

OF FRANKLIN TOWNSHIP

SOMERSET COUNTY

GENERAL ELECTION, NOV. 6, 193

Polls Open From 7 A. M. To 8 P. M.

Paid for by Peter C. S. Hagen

TOWNSHIP TAX COLLECTOR, 1934. Peter C.S. Hageman was Franklin Township's tax collector from 1928 until his death in 1943. Then his widow took over the duties for twenty-four more years. For nearly forty years, the room off the south porch of the Hageman farm on South Middlebush Road served as the tax collector's office (see facing page). Family members were pressured to sell the farm to the state in 1972 for the Six Mile Run Reservoir. In 1978, after vandals threatened the property, the state allowed the township to purchase the buildings. The Meadows Foundation now maintains them.

# *Eight*

# House and Home

GARRETSON-HAGEMAN HOUSE, SOUTH MIDDLEBUSH ROAD, *c.* 1880s.

EMMA VOORHEES HOUSE, BLACKWELLS MILLS, 1904. Much of eastern Blackwells Mills is now owned by New Jersey. The state bought up more than 2,500 acres of township land in the late 1960s and early 1970s for the Six Mile Run Reservoir. Many Franklin farmhouses were in the way and earmarked for destruction.

GEORGE LOGAN HOUSE, FRANKLIN PARK, 1904. Ella, George's daughter, is on the porch steps. The house is typical of many frame-construction houses built in nineteenth-century Franklin: gable ended and five bays wide, it has a center hall and a porch centered on the front façade.

ABRAM VOORHEES HOUSE,
PLEASANT PLAINS, 1904.
Much of the Pleasant Plains
section of Franklin Township is
now being developed as part of K.
Hovnanian's Town and Country
Estates.

DINING ROOM, ABRAM
VOORHEES HOUSE, 1904. In
the days before electronic
entertainment, pianos were as
important in many homes as
television is today. The furniture
and fine textured wallcovering
indicate that this Pleasant Plains
house was a fashionable home.

LOOKING NORTH ON OLCOTT AVENUE, 1930s. Many of these houses were built in Middlebush in the quarter century after the Millstone and New Brunswick Railroad came through in 1854. By 1880, the village had twenty-five residences.

MISS AMANDA'S HOUSE, 1941. Mary Amanda Voorhees spent her entire life in this house on South Middlebush Road in Middlebush and was still living there when this picture was taken. She was the Middlebush Reformed Church organist for forty-five years. The house was one and a half stories when it was built by Joseph Wyckoff around 1842.

RALPH W. THOMSON HOUSE, EARLY 1900s. When Thomson moved to this house at the corner of South Middlebush Road and DeBow Street in 1902, only two Middlebush streets had houses on them. Everywhere else was farmland. Thomson, an avid local historian, wrote a history of Franklin and an autobiography.

JOHN L. TOTTEN HOUSE, 1934. Housing construction in Middlebush was at a standstill from about 1880 until the 1920s, and then building resumed. The Totten house was built on South Middlebush Road in 1921.

MARKET STREET, EAST MILLSTONE, *c.* 1908. When East Millstone was surveyed for the National Historic Register in 1980, 114 village structures were studied. Most are two-story, wood-frame, residential buildings. Major architectural styles used with distinction include Greek Revival, Italianate, Second Empire, and Eastlake.

PACE HOUSE, *c.* 1912. Fire destroyed the Pace house on the corner of Wortman and Amwell Roads in East Millstone in 1928. The fire started in the attic, and no one had the fire-fighting equipment to reach it. Volunteers were helpless to do anything except remove the furniture. The house burned to the ground. The Pace fire was the catalyst for the organization of the Millstone Valley Fire Department soon afterward.

NATHANIEL WILSON HOUSE, BUILT *c.* 1888. Wilson, a local merchant, built this house on Market Street in East Millstone. Later, it was the residence of Dr. Cooper, who had his office there. The cupola is gone now, but the house remains an excellent example of High Victorian Eclectic with its Eastlake porch and entrance and very large brackets along the cornice.

JOSEPH H. OLCOTT HOUSE, BUILT *c.* 1860. Olcott started the distillery in East Millstone in the 1850s. The house, at the intersection of Franklin Street and Amwell Road in East Millstone, is a fine example of Italianate architectural style. It was later occupied by Olcott's daughter Josephine and her husband Moritz Otto Korff.

DEMOTT-METTLER HOUSE. This imposing house once stood near the intersection of Mettlers Lane and Amwell Road in East Millstone. It was the home of Howard DeMott and later of Thomas H. Mettler.

WYCKOFF-GARRETSON HOUSE, BUILT EARLY 1700s. This historic eighteenth-century house on South Middlebush Road was marked for demolition as part of the Six Mile Run Reservoir project. In 1978, the Franklin Township Council purchased the house from the State of New Jersey for $100. The Meadows Foundation now maintains the property.

STEPPING STONES, BUILT 1700s. The original part of the house at the corner of Copper Mine and Canal Roads in Griggstown dates back to the pre-Revolutionary era. Later additions, including a wide verandah, were built in the early 1800s. The house sits above the canal on land that offers a great view of the waterway. A private girls' school operated there during World War II, as part of the Scudder-Collver School of New York City.

JOHN HONEYMAN HOUSE, GRIGGSTOWN, c. 1920s. Honeyman is one of Franklin Township's best-known legends. He is said to have spied for Washington during the American Revolution and to have played a pivotal role in the Battle of Trenton. His house, which still stands on Canal Road, looks much different today than it appears in this early photograph.

ROCKINGHAM, BUILT EARLY 1700s. Rockingham (above) was George Washington's residence briefly in 1783, when the U.S. Congress met in Princeton. In 1896, the house was threatened by nearby quarry operations. The DAR purchased Rockingham, and an association was created to raise money to move and restore it. The house was then relocated a few hundred yards up the hill. In 1957 it was moved a second time; it is now facing a third relocation. Rockingham housed quarry workers who blasted away the hill just below the house. They respected the Blue Room (below) as a shrine to Washington by not using it as their living quarters, thus helping to preserve Rockingham's history.

VAN WICKLE HOUSE, EASTON AVENUE, BUILT 1722. When this National Historic Register house was put up for sale in 1976, real estate developers began eyeing the property. A group of concerned residents formed The Meadows Foundation to save the historic structure. (The name "The Meadows" had long been associated with the house.) The house now belongs to the township and is the setting for many community programs, including the Pumpkin Patch Halloween Party and the Christmas Festival featuring Sinterklaus—the Dutch Santa.

GHOSTLY IMAGE, 1938. While documenting the Van Wickle house on Easton Avenue, a photographer for the Historic American Buildings Survey captured on film this image of a little Dutch girl many believe is the Van Wickle ghost. She is visible on the far left, standing next to the fireplace.

# Acknowledgments

This book could not have been compiled through my efforts alone. I wish to thank the staff of the Franklin Township Public Library for supporting this project, particularly Library Director Lorraine O'Dell and Assistant Director January Adams. Special thanks to my wife, Gina-Marie, for her insights and input. I also want to thank my mother, Jane D. Brahms, for her untiring editorial assistance.

This pictorial history would have been impossible to put together if it were not for the wonderful photographic record of Franklin Township that was created over the years by local photographers such as William W. Tetlow, Martin S. Garretson, G. Clifford Nevius, Steve Goodman, and Elton Wade. Those great photographs needed a written historic record to draw upon. For that information, I am grateful to past and present local historians, including Judge Ralph Voorhees, James P. Snell, Elsie B. Stryker, Ralph Thomson, Laura P. Terhune, James Moise, and Robert S. Mettler.

Special thanks to members of the Franklin Township Bicentennial Committee, Griggstown Historical Society, Meadows Foundation, Raritan-Millstone Heritage Alliance, and Friends of the Pleasant Plains School. I am indebted to the Special Collections and University Archives, Rutgers University Libraries, for permission to use photographs from their collection.

Numerous people lent or gave photographs to this project. Many also assisted in identifying the pictures. Thanks go to John Allen; Pat Bacon; Tony Bianculli; David Cooper; Reverend S. Rae Crawford and Nancy Farber of the Pillar of Fire Church and WAWZ; Margaret Bascom Cron; Dan Flatt of WCTC; Charles Gobac; Steve Goodman; Patricia Grassi; Franklin Police Chief Daniel J. Livak; George Luck; Robert S. Mettler; James Moise; Reverend David Risseeuw of the Six Mile Run Reformed Church; Rose Ann Rosenthal of Temple Beth El; Penny Sherwood; Lou Sincak; F. Lloyd Staats; M. Tomlin; Marie Vajo; Ed Vetter; Frances Voorhees; George and Ruth Wade; and Robert Yuell. Photographs that originated with J. Burtis, E. Voorhees, C. Spangenberg, Mrs. C. Treptow, J. Lupo, C. Petrillo, and the Laird family also were used in the project.

Finally, I wish to dedicate this book to the memory of Councilman John M. "Jack" Shreve, who passed away this year. He was the catalyst for much of the preparation for Franklin Township's bicentennial celebration. We'll miss you, Jack.

Happy 200th Birthday, Franklin Township!